Creative Calligraphy ™

M000308585

For my parents,
who always told me to dream big.

Table of Contents

Introduction

Contrary to popular belief, calligraphy and handwriting are two very different things (although learning calligraphy will help you improve your handwriting). What makes calligraphy unique is the variation of thick and thin lines—the contrast within the letterforms.

I believe that anyone at any age can learn how to write beautiful calligraphy. It just takes practice and patience. I first fell in love with calligraphy and began teaching myself when I was 12, after I found a book at my grandma's house. Maybe you want to learn how to address your own wedding invitations, or maybe you just want to take your snail mail to the next level. No matter what your reason is, it's never too late or too early to learn.

Old-school calligraphy was all about perfection. What I love about modern calligraphy is that it's all about personalization. There are so many different ways you can write the same letter. There are no more strict rules to follow. And flaws are OK—they're even encouraged. Modern, creative calligraphy is all about creating letterforms that fit your own unique style and aesthetic.

This book will teach you everything you need to get started in modern calligraphy. It starts with the basics, because you can't break the rules until you know them. You'll learn all about typography terminology, the anatomy of a nib, how to assemble and prepare your pen, how to hold your pen, how to dip your pen, how to make a stroke, and finally, how to write letterforms and words.

Once you have that down, we'll dive into things like troubleshooting and fun stuff like writing on different mediums. Before you know it, you'll be adding your own stunning touch to envelopes, place cards, stationery, chalkboards and everything in between.

Write on!
Kristara

Designer Bio

Kristara Schnippert has been a calligrapher for over 16 years, after teaching herself broad- and fine-tip calligraphy when she was just 12 years old. Known for her modern take on calligraphy, Kristara has worked with countless couples and corporate clients to incorporate hand lettering into their wedding stationery, event signage and brand identity. Her work has been featured in numerous print and online publications, including *The Knot, Southern Bride, Style Me Pretty, 100 Layer Cake* and *Wedding Chicks*. When she's not teaching workshops or making a huge mess in her studio, she enjoys biking around Houston with her husband, Dan, and their pup, Dallas.

Follow her on Instagram (@kristara) or visit www.kristara.co to see her latest work.

Photo by Carr Cormier Photography

Calligraphy Supplies

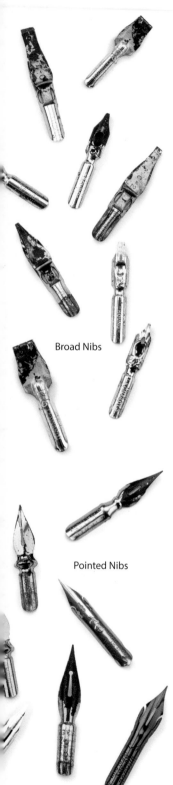

Broad Nibs

Pointed Nibs

Beautiful calligraphy starts with the right supplies. Investing in quality supplies will save you a lot of time and frustration. Every nib, ink and paper has its own unique personality. An ink may write beautifully on one type of paper, but bleed on the next. Certain nibs work best on smooth paper, while others can handle a little more texture. Here are the supplies you'll need to get started.

Nibs

There are two main types of nibs for dip pens. The broad-tip nibs have a chiselled tip, which calligraphers use to write more traditional calligraphy styles like Italic or Gothic. Then there are pointed nibs, which are used to write script styles like the modern calligraphy in this book.

Broad Nibs

To achieve the thick and thin lines in broad-tip calligraphy, you want to position the nib at about a 45-degree angle and not change the angle as you write. The angle can change depending on what particular alphabet you're writing. With broad-tip pens, you also have to pay attention to nib widths, which help you maintain the proportion of your letters. Calligraphy markers and fountain pens all have broad nibs.

Pointed Nibs

Calligraphers use pointed nibs for traditional copperplate and more modern styles of calligraphy. With pointed-pen calligraphy, you get the thick and thin lines by applying pressure to the pen. You also hold these types of pens differently than you do in broad-nib calligraphy. You want to hold the pen at about a 55-degree angle from the horizontal; imagine the point of the tip pointing toward the right corner of your paper. If you're right-handed, this is going to feel a little awkward at first, but I promise you'll get used to it!

Getting to Know Your Pointed Nib

In order to use your nib correctly, it's important to know how your nib works.

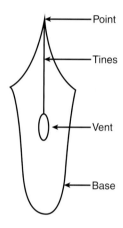

Point

Tines

Vent

Base

Point: The point is critical to getting crisp lettering. A nib's point is very fragile, so you don't ever want to handle your nib by the point. Also, you want to be extremely careful when you're cleaning your pen; if you damage the point, it won't write correctly anymore.

Tines: The tines create the thick and thin lines. When you apply pressure to the tines, they spread apart to give you nice, thick downstrokes. When you release the pressure and glide your pen across the paper, you'll get thin, wispy hairlines. These pressure contrasts are what make pointed-pen calligraphy so beautiful and elegant.

Vent: The small hole in the center of your nib serves as the reservoir for your pen by holding the ink and helping it flow so you're not constantly re-dipping. The vent is important for you to remember because when you dip your pen into the ink, you want to make sure you dip it in just past the vent. In broad nibs, there is an external reservoir that you slide onto your nib to hold the ink.

Base: You always want to grip your nib by the base when you're handling it. Depending on your pen holder, the base may be a little tight or a little loose. I always keep a pair of needle-nose pliers handy to adjust it as needed. Simply squeeze the base a little bit at a time until the fit is right. When you're inserting your nib into the pen holder, you never want to force it in, but you don't want it to be too loose, either.

My Favorite Nibs

It's hard to say which nib is the best, because it's so subjective, but here are the nibs I find myself reaching for the most:

Zebra G Nib

The Zebra G nib was originally used to draw manga art in Japan. It's a fairly stiff nib and great for beginners as you get used to applying pressure.

Brause 361 Steno (Blue Pumpkin) Nib

This nib is a cult favorite, and for good reason. The Blue Pumpkin has medium flexibility and allows you to create fine hairlines and a balanced downstroke.

Hunt 22 Nib

This nib has a unique vintage appeal. It has medium flexibility and a very sharp point, allowing calligraphers to create super-fine hairlines and thick, whimsical downstrokes. The only downside of the sharpness is that it tends to catch if you apply too much pressure on the upstroke.

Brause Rose Nib

The Brause Rose is a strong, yet very flexible nib that almost acts like a paintbrush. This is a more advanced nib that you may want to use once you're comfortable with your calligraphy skills.

A Brief History of Calligraphy

The Evolution of Letters

Before computers, even before printing presses, there was calligraphy. The Roman alphabet has been in existence for over 2,000 years. Over time, these letters have evolved, influenced by social trends, technology and the economic environment.

The Rise of the Codex

Though expensive and difficult to source as they came from Egypt, papyrus scrolls were the most popular writing surface for centuries. They were gradually replaced by the codex, or book. These books were made from parchment and vellum, which were much more durable and versatile materials. This led to the widespread use of the quill pen.

Copperplate Calligraphy

Modern, pointed-pen calligraphy is based on copperplate calligraphy, which rose to prominence after the Renaissance. It was called copperplate because students learning to write this style literally copied from books printed on copper plates. Copperplate calligraphy dominated throughout the 17th century and beyond. Unlike broad-nib calligraphy, copperplate calligraphy uses pressure contrasts to create thick and thin strokes.

Calligraphy Reborn

Today, in a digital world, calligraphy is making a surprising comeback. While computers and fonts are convenient, they often lack personality. Modern calligraphy gives people a way to create beautiful letters, signs and gifts with a human touch—without all the strict rules that come with traditional calligraphy.

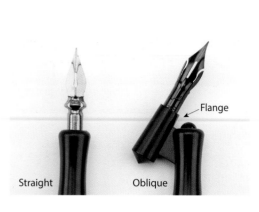

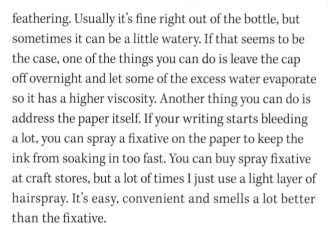

Straight   Oblique   Flange

Pen Holders

To hold your nibs, there are several different pen holder options. If you're right-handed, you'll be using an oblique pen holder with a flange, which was specially created for right-handed people to reach that steep 55-degree angle.

There are also elbow nibs that right-handed calligraphers can put into straight pen holders, but that nib selection is pretty limited. I usually just use straight nibs in an oblique pen holder for the variety and convenience.

If you're a lefty, you'll be using a regular straight pen holder. Lefties are lucky because they are able to reach that angle easily. The only downside for lefties is that they have to be careful about smearing wet ink.

Some modern calligraphers use straight nibs in straight holders, but I find that I have fewer issues if I maintain the 55-degree angle. It also forces you to go outside of your comfort zone and break bad habits.

You can find pen holders in a variety of materials—cork, wood, plastic and glass. I usually use a plastic pen holder; they're inexpensive enough to keep a dedicated nib in so I don't have to constantly switch out nibs.

Ink

My favorite black ink is Higgins Eternal. It's a great professional-grade, general ink that gives you a rich, dense black and fine hairlines. It's nice for beginners because you don't run into a lot of problems like bleeding or

feathering. Usually it's fine right out of the bottle, but sometimes it can be a little watery. If that seems to be the case, one of the things you can do is leave the cap off overnight and let some of the excess water evaporate so it has a higher viscosity. Another thing you can do is address the paper itself. If your writing starts bleeding a lot, you can spray a fixative on the paper to keep the ink from soaking in too fast. You can buy spray fixative at craft stores, but a lot of times I just use a light layer of hairspray. It's easy, convenient and smells a lot better than the fixative.

At the end of the day, ink choice is up to you. A lot of calligraphers swear by India ink or sumi ink. Some people even like to go old-school and use iron gall ink, which was the standard throughout Europe from the 5th century to the 20th century. Iron gall ink has an ethereal, magical quality that transports you back in time.

For beginners, I recommend using non-waterproof ink for best results; it usually just comes in black. As you get more advanced, you can create your own ink in a huge variety of colors by mixing gouache with water until it's the consistency of heavy cream.

> **TIP:** *If you're using thicker ink, if your ink evaporates too much, or if you're mixing your own ink, make sure that you dilute it with distilled water and not tap water until it reaches the consistency of heavy cream. The impurities and bacteria in tap water can react with chemicals in the ink or even cause it to go bad and smell terrible. It's more effort to get distilled water, but it's worth it.*

Paper

Bristol & Watercolor Paper

The best type of paper for calligraphy is thick, smooth paper. In general, look for paper that's at least 70 lb. weight for best results. Bristol paper and watercolor paper are great for calligraphy projects because they don't absorb the ink too fast. When working on thicker paper, give ink enough time to dry as it usually takes longer.

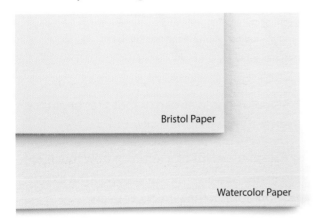

Bristol Paper

Watercolor Paper

Sketch & Copy Paper

Sketch, drawing and copy paper are good for practice only; they tend to bleed. A great paper to practice with is 32 lb. laser-jet paper or a Rhodia notepad. I usually practice a design on cheaper paper before creating the final piece on high-quality paper.

Sketch Paper

Copy Paper

In general, you want to avoid porous, fibrous paper, which makes calligraphy difficult due to excessive bleeding and snagging.

> **TIP:** *A lot of stores carry calligraphy practice pads, but these are surprisingly bad for practicing. They are really meant to help you get used to writing at a slant, which you're not necessarily going to do. You're better off just using computer paper or a notepad.*

Pencils & Erasers

A lot of calligraphy involves sketching or creating your own baseline using a pencil. Make sure you're using a medium-hard artist pencil, such as a 3H or a 4H, or a mechanical pencil. A hard pencil will make pencil lines hard to see and erase completely. A soft pencil will create thick lines that may smudge.

When it's time to erase your pencil marks, make sure you're using a soft white eraser or a kneaded eraser. A white eraser will leave some shreds that you'll need to brush off. A kneaded eraser can be molded into a precise shape and won't leave residue, but they're also a lot softer and may be harder for a beginner to use. Try both and see what your preference is. ●

> **TIP:** *Paper towels don't technically count as equipment, but they're nice to have on hand when writing. Calligraphy is beautiful, but it's a mess behind the scenes. Paper towels are great for blotting up extra ink, removing little fibers that get caught in your nib and wiping your pen.*

Calligraphy Terminology

Ascender: The stroke of a letter that rises higher than the x-height (mid-line) for tall letters like **t** and **l**.

Baseline: The line the words rest upon. In modern calligraphy, a lot of calligraphers follow a moving baseline where the letters bounce above and dip below the baseline.

Bowl: The rounded lines that enclose a counter, or the white space inside an enclosed letter like **b**, **o** or **p**.

Broad Nib: A calligraphy nib with a flat, slanted tip. Broad nibs are not typically used in modern calligraphy styles.

Cap Height: The distance from the baseline to the top of an uppercase letter.

Counter: The white space inside enclosed letters.

Descender: The stroke of a letter that falls below the baseline, as with **y** or **g**.

Flourish: An additional embellishment added to a letter or word to add beauty and visual interest.

Gouache: A vibrant, opaque, water-based paint similar to watercolors. Many calligraphers prefer to mix their own gouache instead of using calligraphy ink.

Pointed Nib: A calligraphy nib with a flexible, pointed tip. Instead of relying on the angle for thick and thin lines, pointed nibs rely on pressure.

Serif: A small, slanted stroke or foot that begins or ends a letter.

Slope: The angle/slant of a letter, or how much the lettering leans. Usually, the more sloped the letters are, the more formal the writing appears.

Tail: A tail is an exit stroke of a letter, such as the final curve in an e.

X-Height: The height of a regular lowercase letter. The x-height is the distance between the baseline and the top of a lowercase x. It's often used to measure contrast between upper and lowercase letters. ●

TIP: *The serifs are especially important to note because these are what you use to connect your letters. When writing words, exaggerate the foot, or exit stroke, of each letter to serve as the connection to the next one.*

Getting Ready to Write

Before you begin writing, there are a few essential things you must learn how to do—like insert your nib into your pen holder and dip your pen into ink.

Insert the Nib

Inserting a nib into a straight holder is relatively easy. It doesn't matter what angle you put the nib in, you just have to ensure that it is in securely. You never want to force it or jam it in too deep; this may cause trouble when dipping the pen, or ink will get inside the pen holder and spill out as you're writing (Photo 1).

You also don't want the nib to be loose or it will wobble and you'll have trouble writing.

If you're using an oblique pen holder, lay your pen flat on a table with the flange on the left side. Then grip your nib by the base and insert it into the top of the pen holder. You want to tweak it until the vent hole is flat at the top. It should not be angled at all (Photo 2).

Prepare the Nib

A lot of people don't realize that new nibs have a film on them. The manufacturers do this to protect the nibs from rust and corrosion, which is a good thing. However, it can also hinder the ink flow and prevent the ink from sticking on the nib properly. There are two main ways to prep your nib: the abrasive method and the flame method.

Abrasive Method

In the abrasive method, use an old toothbrush and some toothpaste or dish soap and scrub the nib with warm water. Be careful not to snap the tines or they will never write the same. Dry the nib thoroughly to keep it from rusting.

Flame Method

For the flame method, use a lighter to run a flame over both sides of the nib for a few seconds on each side. Your pen may get a little discolored, but that's OK. If you didn't apply the flame long enough, you'll know because the ink will bead up on your nib instead of sticking on your nib. If that happens, wipe your nib and run it over the flame for a few more seconds.

Note: Always use caution when using the Flame Method.

> **TIP:** *I always prep my nibs in the pen holders because I think it's easier. This practice ensures that I don't drop the nib down the sink or burn my fingers. It's always better to be safe than sorry.*

Hold the Pen

Hold your calligraphy pen like you would normally hold a pencil. Make sure your fingers are in the groove and that your pen is at about a 45-degree angle from your paper. You also want to make sure that you're not squeezing the pen too tight. You just want to have a light grip on your pen. When you're holding your pen, you want the nib to point toward the right corner of your paper. Feel free to slant your paper slightly to the left to make this easier as you're writing (Photos 3 and 4).

Right-Handed

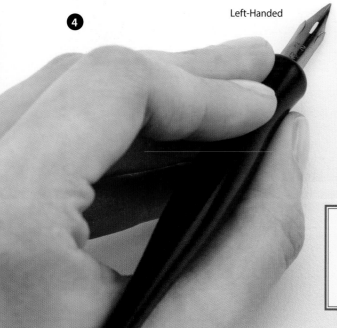

Left-Handed

Stir the Ink

It's very tempting to shake your ink bottle, but try to refrain from doing that. Shaking the ink creates tiny bubbles that can mess up your writing. The great thing about plastic pen holders is that they can double as an ink stirrer! Invert your pen holder and use the handle to stir the ink, then wipe it clean with a paper towel. You want to do this to make sure that the pigment is distributed evenly.

This is especially important when you start using thicker inks or making your own ink using gouache. If you feel like you must shake it, just make sure you wait for the bubbles to settle before you start writing.

Dip the Pen

When dipping the pen, make sure that you dip your pen in the ink just past the vent hole. As you pull your pen back up, brush the nib lightly against the inside edge of the jar to remove excess ink. Take a close look at your nib. If the vent is filled with ink, you're ready to start writing (Photo 5). ●

> **TIP:** *A lot of people don't realize the importance of ergonomics in calligraphy. Any time you're going to be sitting for a long period of time, you'll want to make sure you're maintaining good posture and taking frequent breaks.*

Making Your Mark

As you delve deeper into calligraphy, you'll realize that every letter, numeral and symbol is made up of a combination of similar shapes and strokes. For example, in calligraphy, the letter **a** is like an **o** and an **i** combined. And a **g** is similar to an **a**, but with a longer downstroke. These practice strokes are the building blocks of any alphabet set. Once you've mastered these, you'll be able to write any letter with ease.

Guidelines and practice stroke sheets are provided for you on pages 45–47. Photocopy these sheets. You can then place the guide sheets behind your paper so you can write in a straight line as you're practicing.

Upstrokes

Now that you know what a baseline is, that's where you'll start. Make sure your nib is facing the right corner of your paper—about a 55-degree angle—and slide your pen from the baseline to the cap height line. Don't use any pressure at all; just glide your nib across the paper. You've made your first stroke (Photo 1).

Practice a few more times while making sure you're moving your pen as lightly as possible across the paper. You may be surprised at how light you can go. Try to get your upstrokes as smooth and consistent as possible; pay close attention to the thickness of the stroke and the angle of the line.

> **TIP:** *If your upstroke is a bit shaky, that's OK. Make sure you're moving your whole arm, not just your wrist. Glide your arm across the paper with your pen and your wrist so you have more control over the movement.*

Downstrokes

Once you're comfortable with your upstrokes, it's time to move on to the downstrokes. For this, make sure that you're holding your pen the same way as for the upstrokes. Then gently put a little bit of pressure onto the pen until the tines open up at the same time. Apply smooth, even pressure to the pen as the ink flows out of the nib (Photo 2).

Practice your downstrokes a few more times. It's important to take your time and make sure that you're getting the right angle and consistency. If your downstroke is a bit ragged, you're probably not applying even pressure. Try it again and see how uniform you can get your strokes.

> **TIP:** *A lot of people are afraid of applying too much pressure, but when you first get started, you're probably not applying enough. Go ahead and apply a little more pressure until you see a nice, fat downstroke.*

Combination Strokes

Loop Shape

Create the loop shape by starting with an upstroke. Place the nib at the baseline and move it upward toward the cap height line. Once you've reached the peak of the upstroke, apply gradual pressure while gently pulling your nib downward until you are in your downstroke (Photo 3).

U Shape

Start the U shape, also called the pressure-and-release stroke, by placing your nib at the cap height of your guide sheet. Then gently pull the nib downward while applying pressure and gradually curving to the right. Once you've reached the baseline, relieve the pressure and move your pen upward using your upstroke technique (Photo 4).

Sideways S Shape

The sideways S shape is an extension of the U shape. Start at the cap height of your guide sheet, and then create a downstroke. At the bottom of the downstroke, go into your upstroke. Then, at the peak of the upstroke, apply another downstroke. You can also try the S shape the opposite way by starting with an upstroke, moving to a downstroke and then finishing with another upstroke (Photo 5).

O Shape

The O shape is key to mastering the alphabet. Start at the cap height and move your pen in a counterclockwise motion starting with a downstroke and then moving into an upstroke to close the form. Make sure that the bowl isn't too round or too narrow (Photo 6).

Managing Ink Flow

You'll run out of ink a lot faster during your downstrokes. Look closely at your lines. See how some of them are getting a little transparent? That's how you know you're about to run out of ink.

If you can tell you're running out of ink, go ahead and dip your pen proactively. If you do run out of ink in the middle of a stroke, you can fix it. Just reload your pen and either touch it up with just the point or go over it. This happens all the time, so it's something that you should practice. ●

Troubleshooting

While practicing strokes, you may run into some issues like your pen snagging or the ink not flowing well. Every calligrapher deals with these common issues at one time or another.

Pen Snagging

There are several things you can do to address pen snagging. First, make sure you're writing on smooth paper. Then, double-check that you've prepared your pen properly and are holding it at the correct angle. If you've done both of those things, you may simply be applying too much pressure on the nib—especially on the upstrokes. You may think you're only applying a little pressure, but try going even lighter. Or, if you've been using your nib for a while, it may just be old. Look at your nib closely; if one side of the tip is dull and worn down, it's time to replace it.

Ink Bleeding

If you're noticing that your ink is bleeding or feathering on the paper, try working with the ink first. Is it too watery for the paper? If you think that may be the case, try leaving the cap off overnight so the excess water can evaporate. You can also treat the paper itself. Try creating a barrier on the paper so the ink doesn't soak in as fast. You can use a thin layer of aerosol hairspray or fixative. You can also dab a thin layer of gum sandarac powder on the paper.

The majority of ink bleeding issues can be avoided entirely by using quality paper. Anything too textured, thin or fibrous isn't really suitable for calligraphy (unfortunately, that includes mulberry paper and kraft paper). Remember, paper over 70 lb. weight is best.

Ink Not Flowing

First, make sure that you're taking your time. If you're going too fast, your ink may not be flowing through the pen correctly. If that doesn't work, try dipping, or "kissing" the very tip of your nib into water and making several downstrokes on some scrap paper. If your ink isn't flowing at all, it may be too thick. Dilute the ink with a bit of distilled water to get it to the right consistency. If ink has dried on your nib, sometimes it can be salvaged. Try scrubbing it lightly with an old toothbrush and warm, soapy water.

Shaky Writing

Becoming good at calligraphy takes time. If you're just getting started, don't be too hard on yourself. Most of the time, shaky writing (especially on upstrokes) can be fixed by moving your entire arm instead of just your wrist. Make sure you're writing in a smooth, fluid motion. Most importantly, relax. If you're tense, it will probably show in your writing. ●

small tall slanted

wide bouncy

curly angular

mixed romantic

bold sharp

short wavy narrow

Letters & Symbols

Calligraphers often use a guide sheet beneath their paper in order to keep their writing on a straight line. We'll be using the same technique to practice writing letters. We've provided six different alphabet sets to help you get started. I recommend photocopying the alphabets in this book and then placing your paper on top of an alphabet and tracing a few times. This will give you a better feel for the texture of the paper and the movements of the letterforms. When you feel ready, try writing these letters freehand, looking at them for reference.

Here are some tips to remember as you start practicing writing letters and symbols:

- Don't try to write calligraphy as you would write cursive. Remember, calligraphy is a series of separate, combined strokes. Although a lot of letters look as if they're formed in a single stroke, they're usually created using multiple strokes. Mentally break the letters down into their most basic shapes and strokes. Any thin lines should be an upstroke. Any thick lines should be a downstroke.

- When it comes to writing capital letters, you generally want to start from left to right—unless you're writing letters B, D , F or P. For these letters, begin with the basic swelled downstroke: start with minimal pressure, build pressure and then taper the pressure toward the end. Use this downstroke as the base, building on it to form your desired letter.

- Cross strokes, such as the cross of a lowercase t or capital A, should be treated like an upstroke. Apply no pressure as you cross the downstroke. This also prevents the ink from dragging as you cross the letter. ●

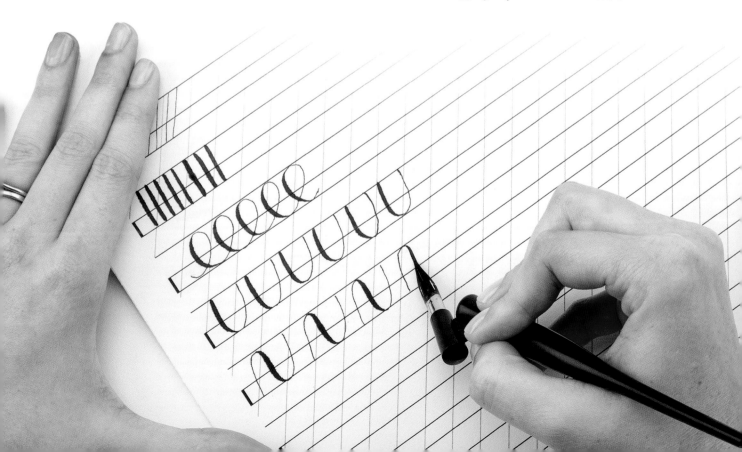

Molly

A B C D E F G H

I J K L M N O P Q R

S T U V W X Y Z

a b c d e f g h i j k l

m n o p q r s t u v w x y z

Logan

A B C D E F
G H I J K L
M N O P Q R
S T U V W X
Y Z

a b c d e f g h
i j k l m n o p
q r s t u v w
x y z

Alexa

A B C D E F G H

I K L M N O P Q R

S T U V W

a b c d e f g

h i j k l m n o

p q r s

Brooke

A B C D E F G H I
J K L M N O P Q R
S T U V W X Y Z

a b c d e f g h i
j k l m n o p q r
s t u v w x y z

Katie

A B C D E F G H
I J K L M N O P
Q R S T U V W
X Y Z

a b c d e f g h i j k
l m n o p q r s t u
v w x y z

Elizabeth

A B C D E F G H I J K L M N O P Q R S T U V W X Y Z

a b c d e f g h i j k l m n o p q r s t u v w x y z

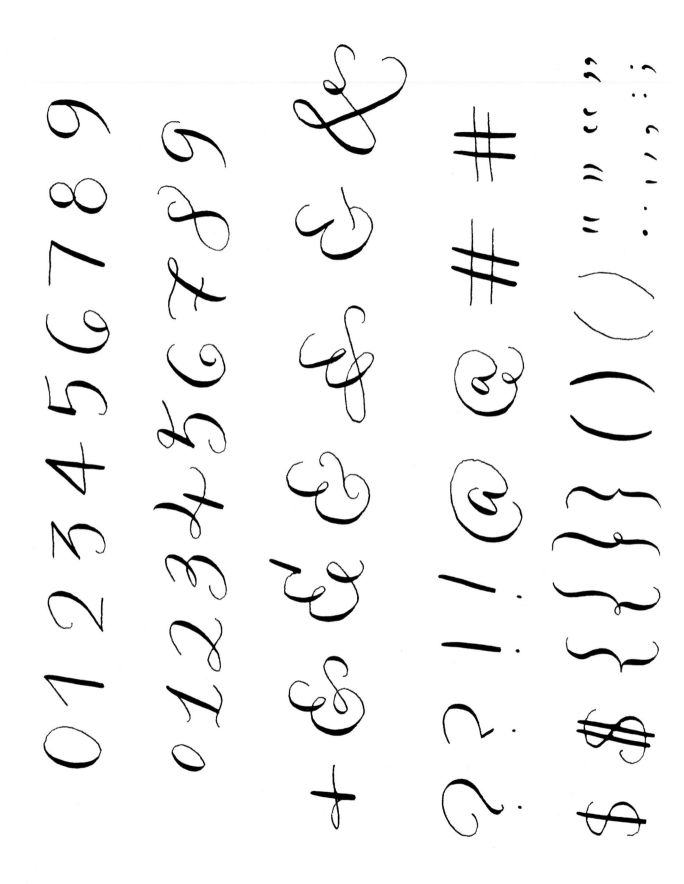

Basic Layouts

Working on Thick or Dark Paper

Once you're comfortable writing letters and words, try writing some sentences. If you're working on thick or dark-color paper that you can't see a guide sheet through, use a ruler to mark dots ½ inch apart on your paper. Then go across and draw a straight line so you have a series of parallel lines. Try writing a paragraph using just a pencil in copperplate style. This should give you an idea of spacing and balance so you can make edits accordingly.

Calligraphy is as much a mental exercise as it is a physical one. You have to think about which letters are coming next and how they all relate and connect to one another. You can save a lot of the flourishes for the end when you can see how the entire composition works together.

Once you're happy with the layout, use your calligraphy pen to go over the pencil. When everything is completely dry, use an eraser to remove the pencil marks.

Addressing Envelopes

You can use the same concept to address envelopes that you use for thick or dark paper. Simply draw the lines lightly in pencil and then erase the pencil marks once the ink is completely dry. Or, if you're writing on a light-color envelope, you can slide the guide sheet inside the envelope and use it to write the address.

When centering the address on the envelope, it's helpful to get an idea of the spacing and length of each line before you begin. Most of the time, it's better to start off a little more to the left than you think necessary, and then adjust the spacing or add a flourish to balance it out. ●

> **TIP:** *When writing words, remember to extend the foot, or exit stroke, of each letter to help it connect to the next one.*

Faux Calligraphy

Pointed-pen calligraphy can only scale up so large while maintaining contrast between the letterforms. When writing on larger mediums like a chalkboard, or unconventional mediums such as wood or stone, you'll need to write faux calligraphy using regular pens and markers. It's more time-consuming than using a dip pen because you have to take more time to fill in the downstrokes, but you can achieve beautiful results with a little patience.

To write in faux calligraphy, write out your message as you would in calligraphy, and then fill in the areas where the downstrokes would be.

Some of my favorite pens for faux calligraphy are:

- uni-ball Gold Gel Pen
- Sharpie® oil-based markers
  (extra fine, fine or medium tips)
- Tombow brush markers
- Copic® markers
- Chalk ink markers

Chalk ink marker

Tombow brush markers

uni-ball gel pens

Sharpie oil-based markers

Copic® markers

Project **Gallery**

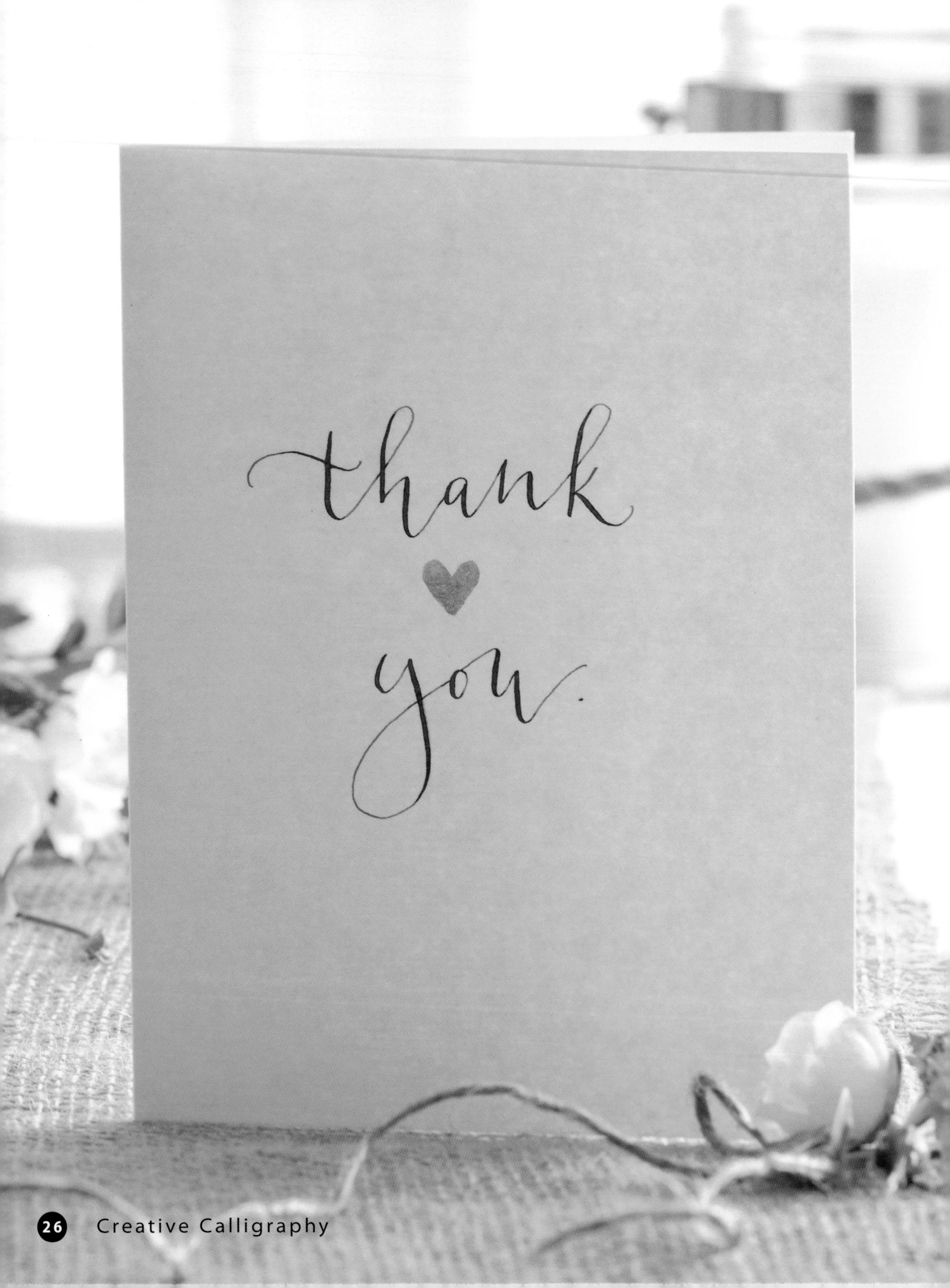
thank
you.

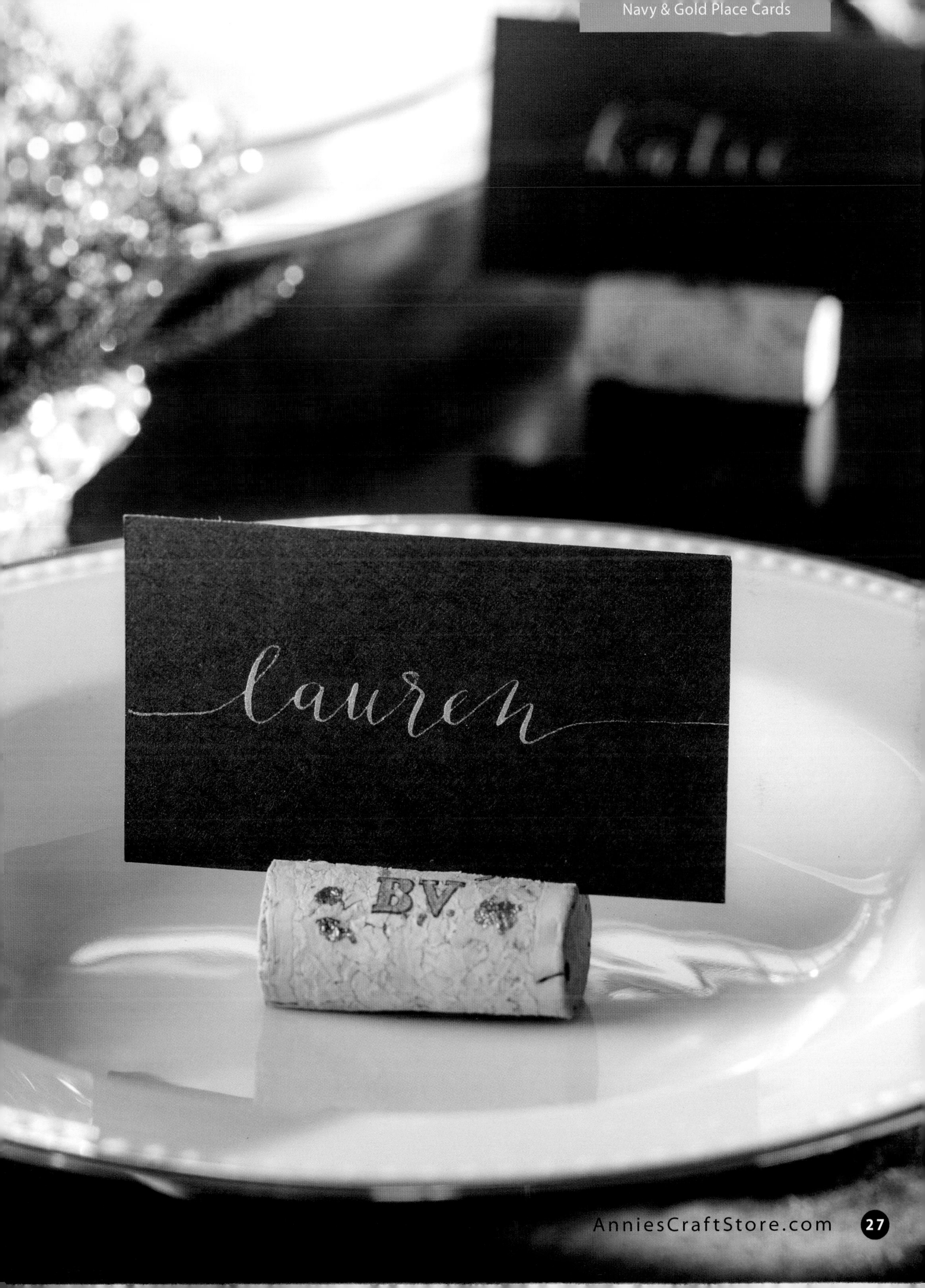
lauren
BV.

menu

first course

GREEK SALAD

TOMATO BASIL SOUP

main

GRILLED TENDERLOIN

CHICKEN MARSALA

EGGPLANT PARMESAN

dessert

PEAR CROSTATA

CHOCOLATE TRUFFLE CAKE

salute

cheers

Skål

Sláinte

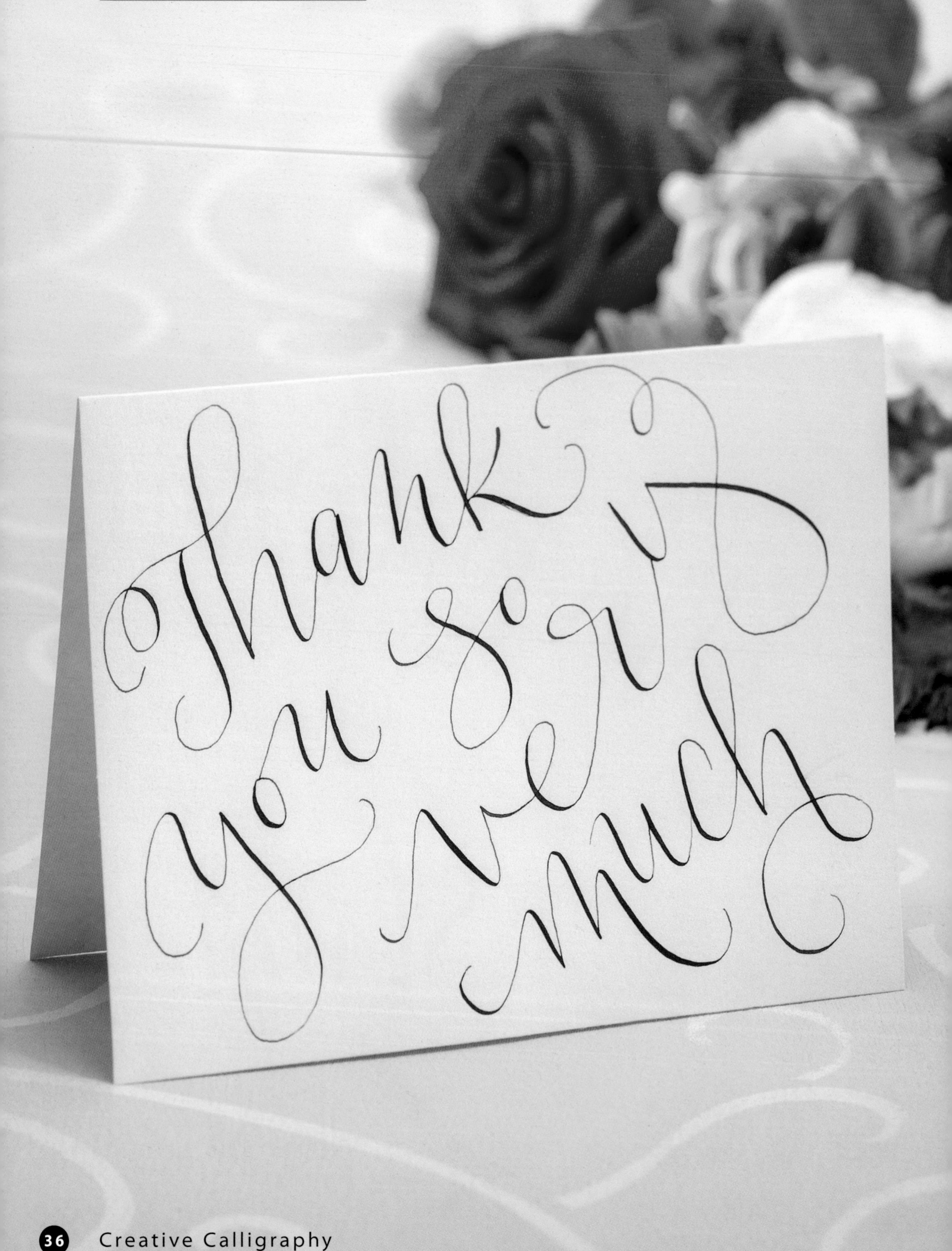
Thank you so very much

mr. and mrs.
Mark Freemon

414 ELM STREET
CHARLOTTE, NC
28209

TOGETHER WITH OUR FAMILIES
WE REQUEST THE PRESENCE
OF YOUR COMPANY
AT OUR WEDDING

Olivia Morgan
and James Craig

MARCH 26, 2016
CHICAGO, ILLINOIS

Vintage postage stamps
from Verde Studio.

congrats

vanilla

lemon

chocolate

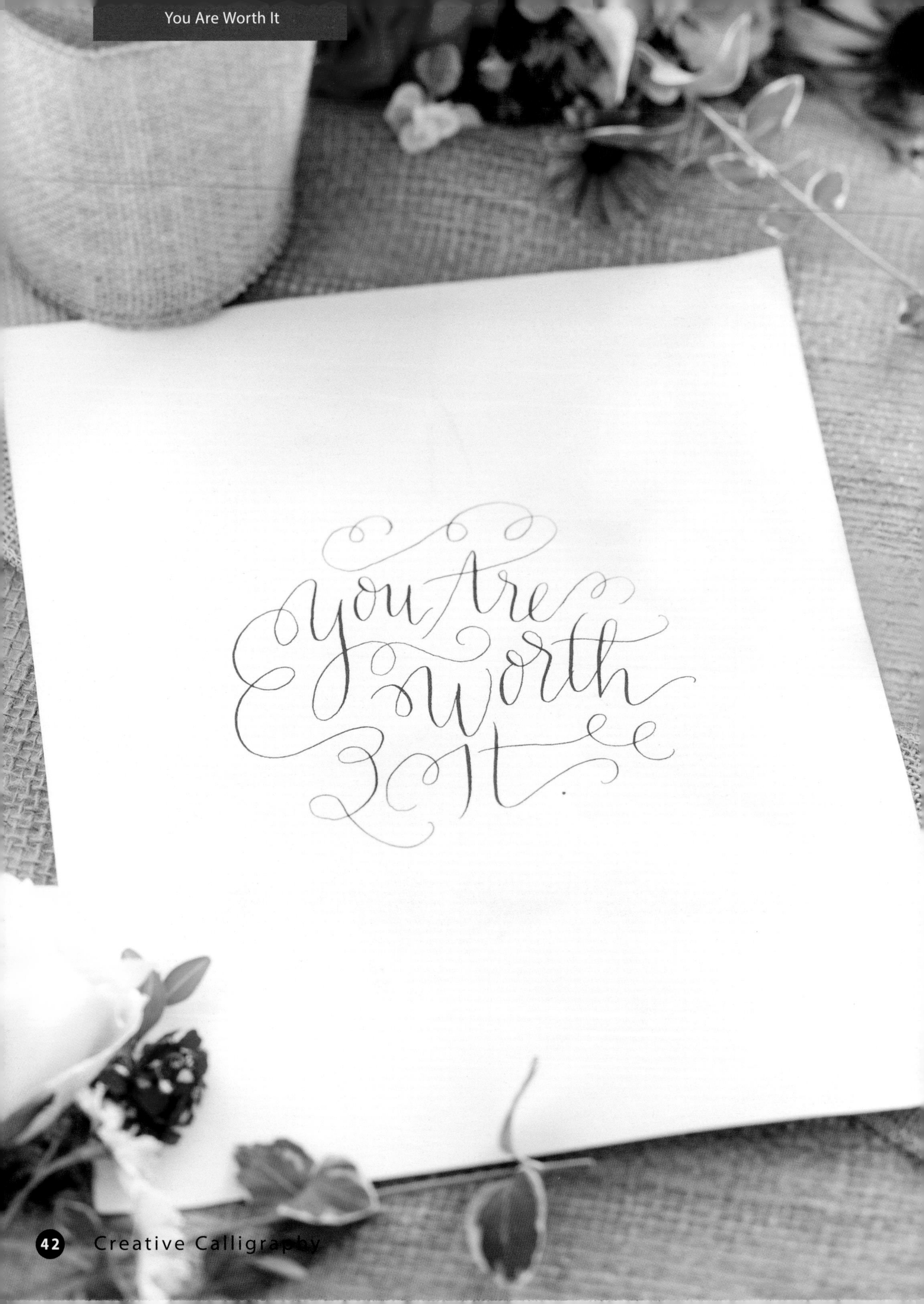
You Are worth It.

menu

APPETIZER

stuffed mushrooms

MAIN COURSE

chicken verona

beef tenderloin

DESSERT

peach crostata

Project Sources

Thank You Card
Page 26
> Cardstock
> Higgins Eternal black ink
> Krylon 18 kt. gold leafing pen
> Zebra Comic G nib
> Pen holder

Navy & Gold Place Cards
Page 27
> Cardstock
> FineTec Arabic gold ink palette
> Hunt 22 nib
> Pen holder
> Paintbrush
> Wine corks

Glitter Birthday Card
Page 28
> Cardstock
> Glitter
> Martha Stewart Crafts glue pen

Birthday Balloons
Page 29
> Cardstock
> Patterned vellum
> Winsor & Newton gouache:
  marigold yellow, opera pink
> Zebra Comic G nib
> Pen holder
> Twine

Gracie Gift Bag
Page 30
> Black paper bag
> FineTec Arabic gold ink palette
> Hunt 22 nib
> Pen holder
> Paintbrush

Wooden Menu
Page 31
> Wood veneer
> Dr. Ph. Martin's Bleed Proof white ink
> Zebra Comic G nib
> Pen holder

Giant Balloon Happy Birthday Card
Page 32
> Cardstock
> Dr. Ph. Martin's Bleed Proof white ink
> Brause Rose nib
> Pen holder
> Twine

Driftwood Place Cards
Page 33
> Driftwood
> Sharpie medium oil-based
  white marker

Gold Gift Tags
Page 34
> Cardstock
> FineTec Arabic gold ink palette
> Zebra Comic G nib
> Pen holder
> Twine
> Paintbrush
> Hole punch

Cork Coasters
Page 35
> Cork coasters
> Sharpie medium oil-based
  black marker
> Acrylic paint
> Paintbrush

Thank You So Very Much Card
Page 36
> Cardstock
> Higgins Eternal black ink
> Zebra Comic G nib
> Pen holder

I Will Always Love You Wooden Sign
Page 37
> Wood with a smooth finish such
  as plywood
> Minwax American walnut wood stain
> Sharpie medium oil-based white
  marker

Wedding Invitation
Page 38
> Cardstock
> Higgins Eternal black ink
> Copic® markers
> Zebra Comic G nib
> Pen holder

Leaf Place Cards
Page 39
> Leaves
> Sharpie medium oil-based
  white marker

Black & White Dessert Toppers
Page 40
> Cardstock
> Dr. Ph. Martin's Bleed Proof white ink
> Zebra Comic G nib
> Pen holder
> Bamboo skewers
> Floral shears
> Hot-glue gun

Gold-Leaf Wooden Coasters
Page 41
> Birch coasters
> White acrylic paint
> Speedball Mona Lisa gold
  leafing sheets
> Krylon 18 kt. gold leafing pen
> Flat paintbrush
> Craft glue

You Are Worth It
Page 42
> Strathmore Bristol paper
> Higgins Eternal black ink
> Brause 361 Steno Blue Pumpkin nib
> Pen holder

Chalkboard Menu
Page 43
> Chalkboard
> Chalk ink marker

Lettering Guidelines Sheet

Lettering Guidelines Sheet

Buyer's Guide

The calligraphy supplies listed in this book can be found at most art supply stores and online at the following websites:

John Neal Bookseller
(800) 369-9598
www.johnnealbooks.com

Paper & Ink Arts
(800) 736-7772
www.paperinkarts.com

Manufacturers

Brause
(800) 933-8595
www.exaclair.com/brands_brause.php

Copic®/Imagination International Inc.
(541) 684-0013
www.imaginationinternationalinc.com

Dr. Ph. Martin's
(800) 843-8293
www.docmartins.com

FineTec
www.finetec-mica.de

Higgins
(800) 628-1910
www.higginsinks.com

Krylon
www.krylon.com

Martha Stewart Crafts
www.eksuccessbrands.com/marthastewartcrafts

Minwax
(800) 523-9299
www.minwax.com

Rhodia
(800) 933-8595
www.rhodiapads.com

Sharpie
(800) 346-3278
www.sharpie.com

Speedball
(800) 898-7224
www.speedballart.com

Strathmore Artist Papers
www.strathmoreartist.com

Tombow
(800) 835-3232, ext. 511
www.tombowusa.com

uni-ball
(800) 346-3278
www.uniball-na.com

Verde Studio
www.verdestudio.etsy.com

Winsor & Newton
www.winsornewton.com

The Buyer's Guide listings are provided as a service to our readers and should not be considered an endorsement from this publication.

Annie's®

Creative Calligraphy is published by Annie's, 306 East Parr Road, Berne, IN 46711. Printed in USA. Copyright © 2015, 2016 Annie's. All rights reserved. This publication may not be reproduced in part or in whole without written permission from the publisher.

RETAIL STORES: If you would like to carry this publication or any other Annie's publication, visit AnniesWSL.com.

Every effort has been made to ensure that the instructions in this publication are complete and accurate. We cannot, however, take responsibility for human error, typographical mistakes or variations in individual work. Please visit AnniesCustomerService.com to check for pattern updates.

ISBN: 978-1-57367-826-1
2 3 4 5 6 7 8 9